NEW JERSEY

AN AMERICAN PORTRAIT

The Great Falls in Paterson. (Joyce Ravid)

NEW JERSEY

AN AMERICAN PORTRAIT

APRIL BERNARD
& LUC SANTE

KATHLEEN KLECH
PHOTO EDITOR

LYNN HAZLEWOOD
DESIGN

A ROUNDTABLE PRESS BOOK

TAYLOR PUBLISHING COMPANY
DALLAS, TEXAS

A ROUNDTABLE PRESS BOOK

Editorial: Marsha Melnick, Susan E. Meyer
      Marguerite Ross, John Sturman
Photo Editor: Kathleen Klech
Assistant Photo Editor: Anja Hübener
Book and Jacket Design: Lynn Hazlewood
Map (page 7):   Oliver Williams
Front Cover Photo: Jan Staller
Back Cover Photo: Len Jenshel

Library of Congress Cataloging in Publication Data

Bernard, April.
    New Jersey: an American portrait.

    1. New Jersey—Description and travel—1981—
—Views. 2. New Jersey—History—Pictorial works.
I. Sante, Luc.   II. Title.
F135.B43 1986   974.9   86-6004
ISBN 0-87833-540-4

Printed in the United States of America
10 9 8 7 6 5 4 3 2 1

First published in 1986 by Taylor Publishing
Company, 1550 W. Mockingbird Lane,
Post Office Box 597, Dallas, Texas 75221

In the Hoboken train station. (Jan Staller)

NEW JERSEY

State Motto: Liberty and Prosperity

Nickname: The Garden State

Flower: Purple Violet

Bird: Eastern Goldfinch

Animal: Horse

Tree: Red Oak

Insect: Honeybee

Population (1981): 7,404,000

Density (1980): 986.2 per square mile

Households: 2,548,594

Counties: 21

Municipalities: 567

Manufacturing Establishments (1982): 13,910

Farms (1982): 9,500

Highways and Roads: 33,077

Area: 8,204.37 square miles

Land Area: 7,504.8 square miles

Water: 699.57 square miles

Length (greatest point): 166 miles (High Point to Cape May)

Width (narrowest point): 32 miles (Trenton to Raritan Bay)

Highest Point: 1,803 feet (High Point)

Atlantic Coastline: 127 miles

Oliver Williams

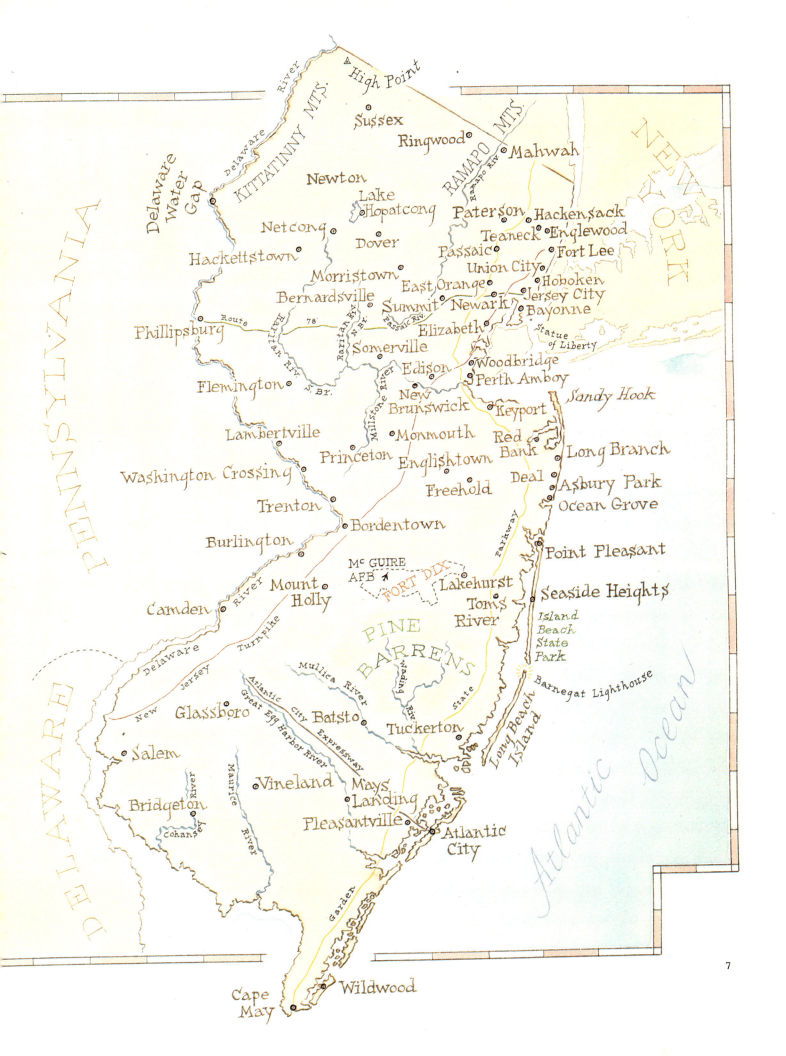

CONTENTS

ON THE MOVE   15

COMMUNITY   33

THE GARDEN   61

AT WORK   85

THE SHORE   105

AT PLAY   125

THE PAST IN THE PRESENT   149

INTO THE FUTURE   167

INDEX   182
PHOTOGRAPHY CREDITS   183

The old carousel in Asbury Park. (Len Jenshel)

FOREWORD

This is a portrait of a state—not a formal one in oils, but more of a charcoal sketch. It is, after all, not meant to stand in for the experience of New Jersey but to suggest it, to whet the appetite.

We have logged much time and gasoline on the big and small roads of New Jersey. In addition, half our team spent his formative years in the state. Our experiences have filled us with affection for New Jersey, if not blind love, and our writing no doubt reflects this. We admire New Jerseyans, but not everything they do. Our task is not boosterism—there are chambers of commerce and boards of tourism for that—but the less accommodating task of social anatomy. The photographs speak for themselves.

When the great photographer Henri Cartier-Bresson was asked to do a photographic essay on the United States a few years ago, he spent most of his time in New Jersey. When asked why, he responded, "New Jersey *is* America." We think so, too.

April Bernard
Luc Sante

Overleaf: PA Tech, a research, development, and consulting firm, has its North American headquarters in Hightstown. It is one of many high-tech firms that makes its home in New Jersey. (Otto Baitz)

11

ON THE MOVE

It must be acknowledged at the outset that New Jersey has an inferiority complex. The state's size, fourth smallest in the Union, and location, smack between the behemoths of New York City and Philadelphia, have a great deal to do with its self-image as a beleaguered "little guy." Then there are the New Jersey jokes. Central to this dubious form of humor is the perception of the state as an industrial cesspool wherein dwells the very middle of banal middle America. Yet the jokes may derive from a tradition that far predates their current incarnation as lame patter on late-night television talk shows. As long ago as 1695, William Penn found it necessary to spring to the region's defense (where, not coincidentally, he had also invested heavily in real estate). "That there is such a province as New Jersey

A state of motion: By foot, by plane, by train, by bus, and especially by car, New Jersey is constantly on the move. Cars speed along the scenic Garden State Parkway; a boy hurries home for supper. (Opposite: Ken Robbins; Left: Larry Fink)

is certain," he wrote home to England. "That it is reputed of those who have travelled in that country, to be wholesome of air and fruitful of soil, and capable of sea trade, is also certain; and it is not right in any to despise or dispraise it."

Clearly, calumny was in the air long before relative size or locale could have engendered it. Wise folk in New Jersey can, though perhaps with no small effort, embrace misunderstanding and dispraise as a kind of birthright—a spur to virtuous high-mindedness, rather than a source of shame. On the other hand, when nonresident wags insist that one's state animal is Miss New Jersey, tempers may fray.

Whatever the deep cause of the problem, history has only reinforced it. Those cow towns to the immediate northeast and southwest did grow into mighty metropolises, and New Jersey became a well-trodden middle-ground, the road taken. With familiarity came affection and contempt in equal measure. The state certainly took its licks during the Revolutionary War, when armies colonial, British, and Hessian stomped across it on their bloody ways between the big cities. And as trading expanded in the years after the war, New Jersey's ceaseless provision of food and ore prompted Benjamin Franklin to observe that the state was "a barrel tapped at both ends." It still is.

If America as a whole is restless, then New Jersey is hyperactive. In 1640, the first wagon road in the colonies was cut to copper mines in the Kittatinny Mountains. The first steam ferry anywhere in the world was launched by Colonel John Stevens from Hoboken to Manhattan in 1808; in 1870, the first asphalt road was laid in the port city of Newark. Though the Wright brothers flew on the winds of Cape Hatteras to the south, the first commercial airline was in New Jersey. Shortly after the Second World War, the first cloverleaf, that engineering miracle beloved of highway departments and small children with race-car kits, was erected in Woodbridge.

The New Jersey Turnpike, as it runs 113 miles northward amid petroleum- and chemical-processing plants, spitting automobiles through the tunnels and over bridges into Manhattan, functions as a double-edged symbol. The rewards and poisons of industrialism. The glory of the open

Although only 940 of the state's thousands of miles of track are now in actual use and its eight or nine lines have been consolidated into a single entity—Conrail—railroads remain an important aspect of life in New Jersey. All railroads lead to Hoboken, it seems, and here, in the snowy Hoboken yard, the Dover, Gladstone, and Montclair lines converge. (Armand Agresti)

Vast quantities of produce and mineral resources are still carted by train and truck from New Jersey to the urban centers of the Northeast. Left: Empty boxcars wait for spring under the monstrous skeleton of the Pulaski Skyway in Kearney. Above: The Empire State's symbol of prowess is eyed with suspicion by those on the Secaucus side of the Hudson River. (Both: Jan Staller)

Overleaf: The giant to the north, New York City, is both a blessing and a curse, a friend and a foe. (Joe Maloney)

road and the desecration of nature. Personal liberty and social alienation.

But the beautiful and aptly named Garden State Parkway, on the other hand, conveys the pleasure of travel unmixed with pain. Running the length of the state, from the New York state line all the way to Cape May, the parkway's rolling curves and careful landscaping show what highways ought to be. And the majestic sweep of the Pulaski Skyway—which affords the humble automobile driver the heady, albeit slightly nauseating, sensation of actually being airborne over the Passaic River and marshlands—is a modernist masterpiece. Indeed, no architect of the Appian Way could have been more drunk with power than was New Jersey's highway department in the 1950s and '60s—stretching and stacking and crossing and looping and bending and merging hundreds upon hundreds of miles of asphalt along the dotted lines.

That creaky one-act play, by Thornton Wilder, *The Happy Journey to Trenton and Camden* (at one time inflicted on elementary-school dramatics classes the nation over) says it all: America *is* the nuclear family out for a Sunday drive in New Jersey.

Meanwhile, New Jersey's major airports—Newark International, Teterboro, and Atlantic City—do a brisk business, too. Aside from the explosion of the *Hindenburg* in 1937—and those crates of jelly jars that fell inexplicably from an airplane taking off from Newark a few years ago—New Jersey's air travel has a reputation for relative smoothness and lack of incident.

The state's railroad system was once a remarkable nerve net of tracks to every conceivable township. The dominion of the highway system in recent years may make it hard to believe that in the mid-nineteenth century, a railroad monopoly, the Camden and Amboy Company, virtually ran the state. (The company's dominion was shattered eventually by antitrust legislation, and many additional companies quickly began to lay track.) A few major lines still run—on only about nine hundred miles' worth of what was once tens of thousands of miles of track. Amtrak sails through on its path between Boston and Washington, D.C. A branch of Conrail—once the venerable Erie-Lackawanna, an amalgam of two formerly independent lines—still regularly trundles commuters to and from the bedroom communities of the Northeast.

When Caesar's Atlantic City was under construction, these colorful hoardings disguised the less-than-beautiful building process with an advertisement for the casino and hotel complex to come. Meanwhile, two senior citizens pursue one of the city's remaining outdoor recreations. (Bob Krist)

The majestic sweep of the Lincoln Tunnel entrance, and the great columns from which the George Washington Bridge is suspended, aptly frame two of the state's important doors, through which much of the Northeast corridor's traffic must eventually pass. (Above: John Kennard; Right: Brian Rose)

One of New Jersey's identities is that of the prototypical commuter state. For decades, citizens have fled the cities for the sweet countryside of New Jersey, where the living was easier and the property taxes lower. The results of that exodus are plain today. Although many New Jerseyans of course work in the communities where they live, hundreds of thousands of their fellows leave every morning for Philadelphia or New York by train, bus, and car.

Like a giant organism, the state every morning exhales its commuting laborers, only to inhale them back again at night. A kind of patience, a long-suffering bred in the very bowels of the landscape, is almost audible: a great, heaving sigh of relief as the gray suits march away, and a forgiving sigh of resignation, even love, when they return, weary, in the twilight.

Left: Chemical explosions have plagued New Jersey in recent years. Perhaps the most spectacular was this 1983 oil refinery fire in Port Elizabeth.
Top: A distinctive railroad bridge over the Passaic River near Newark.
Above: A freight spur near a meadowlands factory. (All: Armand Agresti)

Opposite: A ghostly train departs from the Hoboken station of the PATH line. (Nancy Sirkis)
Left: The stately Morris Goodkind Memorial Bridge spans the Raritan River. (John Kennard)
Below: Tracks crosshatch the snow in the meadowlands near Harrison. (Ray Mortenson)

Overleaf: By no means is all of New Jersey's travel earthbound. (Joel Sternfeld)

COMMUNITY

In 1664, the Duke of York awarded the land between the Hudson and Delaware rivers to John, Lord Berkeley, and Sir George Carteret. A decade or so later, after a certain amount of confusion and infighting, this territory was divided in two. Carteret kept the eastern share, while the west was granted to a group of Quakers, associates of William Penn. A deed drawn up in 1676 illustrated the division: the boundary ran northwest from Little Egg Harbor to a spot north of the Delaware Water Gap. The halves were reunited in 1702, but a breach within the future state had been created, and it would never entirely go away.

Today the split looks a bit different, rather more latitudinal than longitudinal. The boundary line will be forever in dispute. Some would

A graceful Art Nouveau lamppost in Deal; a large Italian-American family in Elizabeth. (Opposite: Robin Holland; Left: Alex Webb/MAGNUM)

place it roughly between Bordentown and Perth Amboy; others would tip it the other way, northeast along the area-code line. This division between "Jersey" and "South Jersey" is mostly psychological. There is not much of a language difference, unless you take note of South Jersey's slight drawl and the metropolitan slurring of r's in the North. The split has somewhat more to do with economics, the North being identified with its industrial belt and the South with its farms. It has even more to do with image and identification. The North lies within the dense gravitational field of New York City; the South relaxes in the gentler orbit of Philadelphia and Wilmington, with a suggestion of the Mason-Dixon line.

Within the divisions there are subdivisions. The resident of Summit might feel closer to Morristown than to nearby Plainfield, for example, while the state's northwest corner may not feel much like associating with Paterson, and the shore communities have their own very distinct identity and stay aloof from everybody. It may seem strange that so small an entity would be so eager to break itself up even further, but this is merely a reflection of the state's extraordinary diversity. New Jersey in some ways is

Populous Hudson County welcomes successive generations of immigrants to its crowded but colorful accommodations. Housetops in the Hoboken half-light; a reservoir for the population of Weehawken. (Left: Jon Eric Jensen; Above: John Kennard)

a patchwork, a cluster of communities. There is a certain flux in the population due to the enforced relocation of executives from one part of America to another, but this kind of movement is statistically insignificant. Numbers have shown that the more important ebbs and flows occur entirely within the state. New Jerseyans are nothing if not loyal.

New Jersey has harbored as many ethnic groups as have passed through Castle Garden, Ellis Island, and JFK International. Every time one group is so established that it becomes assimilated beyond recognition, another arrives to set down roots. The oldest integral community is in the Pine Barrens, where an English-Scottish-Irish settlement, with black and Native American minorities, has lived for more than 200 years. Elsewhere there are clusters of Irish, Italians, Jews, Slavs, Greeks—groups old enough to be scattered all over the state. Still, most were still localized a mere generation or two ago, and their churches and watering holes, those two infallible

indicators, still survive. There is the Greek Orthodox cathedral in Asbury Park, the German taverns of Hoboken, Irish spas in Dunellen and Scotch Plains, prominent synagogues in Englewood and Teaneck, Italian churches and restaurants without number. Ethnic enclaves get passed along to new groups as they are abandoned by the old: the Ironbound section of Newark, once Jewish and Italian, has become largely Hispanic, and the same is true of the historically Irish and Polish districts of Jersey City. The torch of assimilation is passed along with the turf, and successive generations spread out in wider rings through the state.

There are also colorful pockets created by smaller and newer groups, still banded together in the wilderness of the new world. Union City, for example, has become almost entirely Cuban in the last quarter-century, with Spanish spoken universally, and its sphere of influence has spread north to Weehawken and West New York. The Japanese colony is

In New Jersey, velocity is highly valued. Left: Teenagers, temporarily immobile, anticipate the pleasures of watching professionals drive very fast at Englishtown Raceway. Above: A quiet suburban street on the outskirts of Paterson just begs for skid marks. (Both: Joe Maloney)

Overleaf: A grand country home in the Victorian style so prevalent in the state. (Henri Cartier-Bresson/MAGNUM)

strongest in Fort Lee, where it runs, among other things, a UHF television station. There are Syrian Jews in Deal, Portuguese in Highlands. At Rova Farms in Jackson, there is a minutely realized reproduction of a Russian village.

It is easy to forget how many New Jersey towns began as specialized communities. The utopian fervor of the last century has left its marks on the present, although the signatures have faded. The best known of these communes was probably the Fourierist Phalanx in Red Bank, which lasted for half a century and produced Alexander Woolcott, as well as a fine-looking old hotel that burned down in the early 1970s. Colonia and North Stelton are just two of several towns that began as communal experiments. Religious communities also expanded into nonsectarian towns. Methodists founded Ocean City and Ocean Grove, Lutherans settled Oldwick, and Moravians established Hope. The first Jewish farm settlement in the United States was founded at Alliance in the 1880s. One community that is still active is Zarephath, run by the Pillar of Fire Society, which manages a theological college, newspaper, and radio station, as well as the town's post office and fire department.

But communities today are more likely to be centered around economic and social bonds than idealistic concerns. New Jersey possesses every sort of American community. At one end of the statistical curve are the rich. There are the rural centers of wealth, such as Bernardsville and Basking Ridge, where men and women in red jackets and white breeches still ride to hounds in the autumn. There are also the tremendously rich suburbs like Short Hills and Rumson, examples of the bedroom community raised to its Platonic ideal, with sprawling Tudor split-levels, perfect lawns, teenagers who drive expensive foreign cars, and malls that routinely sell Italian shoes, Belgian chocolates, and Chinese dogs. At the other extreme are the desperately poor cities that, for all the talk of restoration and renewal, are far from emerging from the tight corner into which they were pushed a generation ago, when the middle-class exodus began. Rents are soaring in Hudson County as the overflow from Manhattan demands picturesque urban dwellings, but the poor are merely pushed farther out toward the fringes of the metropolitan radius. The once great city of Newark remains a study in decay, and the industrial towns—Bayonne, Elizabeth, Irvington—have been similarly left to rot. Even worse off is the city of Camden,

The first baseball game was played in New Jersey in 1846. Ever since, New Jersey kids have been developing aim and stamina in sandlot leagues, and this game in Point Pleasant Beach carries on the long tradition. (John Kennard)

formerly a shipbuilding center, which has practically no industry left at all. In such places the notion of community means the human resources which are all that remain when material prospects have run out.

Somewhere in the middle lies the typical New Jersey community. This half-mythical place is essentially suburban, but it retains many rural features. It was founded and named in the eighteenth century but developed substantially only after the Second World War. It has a fairly small business district, which has been further reduced over the past decade by the popularity of the mall on the highway. It possesses one parochial school and three public elementary schools, a high school, a diner, two bars on the edge of town and a dressed-up cocktail lounge near the center, four gas stations, and a tennis club. There are a number of factories lined up on the back road out of town, although two of these have had to close recently. Most of the town's residents own their own homes. These range from a few spacious Victorians on the main street, through a large tract of smallish Cape Cods from the early 1950s, to a furious hothouse development of big split-levels built in the last fifteen years, lined up in tiers on the formerly

less accessible hills behind the town. There is one road which until recently was entirely taken up by small farms, but not long ago a garden apartment complex was built at one end, and it was an enormous financial success. More such complexes are planned, and they are expected gradually to replace all the farms.

Most of the town's inhabitants are third- or fourth-generation white ethnics. There are remains of a specific immigrant enclave near the town's center, but the separateness of that community has been mostly eradicated, with only a restaurant, a bakery, and a social club standing as markers of the past. The town has a sleepy town council that fights furiously over the budget each year and then disappears. The most visible political manifestation in town is the board of education, which holds heated biweekly sessions during the school year. Otherwise, there is not much public life. The Memorial Day parade was discontinued in the 1960s, and the Fourth of July fireworks, run by the fire department, remains the one occasion when most everyone in town can be counted on to be present. Teenagers congregate in the parking lot of the burger joint out by the gas stations.

Diners are a ubiquitous feature of the New Jersey roadscape, outwardly scorned by snobs but secretly beloved of all. Rosie's Diner, built in 1935, is a classic example of roadside Moderne, with its glass bricks and Art Deco trim. Rosie's has achieved national fame as the locale for the Bounty paper towel commercials on television. The Leaning Tower of Pizza, on Route 22, embodies the liberating architectural folly of the 1950s and '60s, a style that enlivened many drab highways with overstatement. (Both: Harvey Wang)

Ocean Grove is a unique shore community. Once a strictly devout Methodist enclave, it has recently allowed an influx of nonbelievers. Every summer, though, it reverts to its century-old role, as thousands of pilgrims arrive from around the country to dwell temporarily in tent houses erected on wooden foundations. (Above: Diane Repp) Ocean Grove's Auditorium, an 8,000-seat building at the head of Pilgrim's Pathway, hosts youth rallies, visiting evangelists, and all manner of fervent assemblies. (Opposite: Curt Richter; Overleaf: John Margolies/ESTO)

Almost everyone over eighteen has a car, most families having one per member. Only one street has sidewalks. Accidents are frequent on the two highways leading into town. The town has one celebrated native son, a professional football player.

According to a 1981 estimate based on the 1980 census, New Jersey has approximately 7,404,000 inhabitants, divided among 2,548,594 households. In 1980 the state had a concentration of 986.2 souls per square mile, giving it the greatest population density of the 50 states. New Jerseyans are thickly spread over 21 counties and 567 municipalities. These smaller units range in size from tiny hamlets at crossroads to giant unincorporated townships that spread across the countryside. Presiding over all is the governor, who is elected to a four-year term, according to the revised state constitution of 1949. He can be re-elected once, and if he wishes to try for a third term he must wait out one full electoral cycle. Representing the state

in Washington are fourteen congressmen and the standard pair of senators. The bicameral state legislature is composed of a senate of forty members and an assembly of eighty. These meet in the State Capitol complex on West Street in Trenton, a hive that also includes, besides government offices, a museum, a library, and a planetarium.

Over the years, New Jersey has been alternately Democratic and Republican, with neither party dominating for very long. This has been true from the beginning, even in the heated Lincoln-Douglas contest of 1860, when the state electoral vote was split. New Jersey was mostly Democratic in the late nineteenth century, but then went overwhelmingly for the Republican presidential candidate William McKinley in 1896. By contrast, its most prominent local politician, Woodrow Wilson, who served as president of Princeton University and governor of the state before acceding to the White House, was a Democrat. In the twentieth

T-shirts are a major medium of communication among teenagers everywhere. Here, an alumnus of Rock 'n' Roll High School tends a concession in Asbury Park, and a proponent of Coca-Cola (in Hebrew) augments his allowance by blowing leaves off lawns in Summit. (Opposite: Joe Maloney; Above: Jeff Weiner)

The state's early industrialization, combined with its history of tolerance, have made it a natural resting place for flocks of immigrants from overseas. Italians, Poles, Irishmen, Germans, Russians—and, most recently, Asians—have settled into distinctive communities. Adaptation and traditionalism have blended to create enclaves such as that of the Japanese in Fort Lee—Mets fans and entrepreneurs who maintain a bilingual heritage. (All: Bob Krist)

On a rural road between Cassville and Jackson stands Rova Farms, a 1,400-acre spread developed by Russian émigrés. Under the auspices of the Russian Consolidated Mutual Aid Society, it has become a retirement community that preserves the character of a Russian village, surrounded by farmlands and woods. Opposite: Maria Morozoff sells leeks from the back of a truck. Behind her looms St. Vladimir's Church. Above: Elizar Giluchow displays his handsome walking stick, anticipating an evening of games of chance, in which an Elvis tapestry figures as an unlikely prize. (Both: William Coupon)

century, the state has nearly always gone with the majority in national elections. This relative disregard of party differences was refined by Frank Hague, the mayor and, for all intents and purposes, owner of Jersey City in the 1920s and '30s, who worked both parties simultaneously and indiscriminately. This inspired the *New York Times* to comment: "If most politics is queer, New Jersey politics is queerer."

New Jersey has not been the purest of states, politically speaking. Hudson County in particular has had a checkered history, giving the world not only Hague, a boss of the stature of Huey Long and Richard Daley, but, more recently, another mayor of Jersey City, the notorious Anthony Impelliteri. Other corrupt state denizens include former Labor Secretary Raymond Donovan, former Senator Harrison "Pete" Williams, and a host of other Abscam fingerees. The long and tangled history of cooperation between governmental forces and organized crime may be coming to an end. It is to be hoped that the current cleanup of the environment under way in the state be thorough, and that it define "pollution" in the broadest sense.

The state is in a process of transition these days. One could, in fact, correctly say that it has been so for the past 300 years. The current changes, however, are of a particularly dramatic and far-reaching nature. It is a commonplace to say that rural America is on the verge of a thorough reorganization, and this is as true in New Jersey as anywhere. Failing farm economics are meeting the increasing price of land, and the result is the building of more managerial and research facilities in formerly bucolic areas. Furthermore, New Jersey's highways have been undergoing major changes. The construction of Interstates 80 and 237 and the imminent completion of 78 have transformed the north-central part of the state, instantly suburbanizing vast sweeps of the countryside. To top it all off, the *Mount Laurel* decision of 1985 will affect even the most remote communities. This legislative mandate disallows the minimal acreage zoning regulations that once kept farmlands intact and rich rural towns exclusive. The decision stipulates that all communities must permit and facilitate the construction of lower- and middle-income housing facilities. In theory, this sounds utopian, but in reality it means the likelihood of a weedlike proliferation of jerry-built condominium complexes. Megalopolis is not community, and this is a very serious threat to the state's well-being.

Good fences make good neighbors—and they also contribute to the subtle geometric interplay of shapes in this suburban Passaic County landscape.
(Joe Maloney)

New Jersey possesses a staggering array of foods fast and slow. Opposite: The Red Tower in Plainfield is a survivor of a bygone era of take-out. (George Tice) Above: Giorgio's in Hoboken represents the state's rich Italian culinary heritage, which encompasses everything from the most delicate pastries to the heftiest pizza pie. (Jon Eric Jensen) Left: Pizza goes with New Jersey like gumbo goes with Louisiana. Sal's Pizza in Roselle Park continues the tradition. (George Tice)

Overleaf: The best long-distance swimmers in the country assemble at 6:30 A.M. for the annual Island Swim, which circumnavigates Atlantic City—more than 20 grueling miles. (William Suttle)

THE GARDEN

"The Garden State," New Jersey's nickname, may be best remembered to residents and visitors alike on, ironically, license plates. Given the dominion of the car and the condominium, it may be difficult for some to realize that in fact the state can still lay claim to its moniker, in two different senses. First, agriculture continues to be a major business for small farmers and agribusiness conglomerates. Second, the garden connotes a pristine world, and parts of New Jersey are still preserved in an original, Edenic condition.

Native Americans grew corn, pumpkins and other gourds, tobacco, and

The fields and woods of Somerset and Passaic counties. (Opposite: Jan Groover; Left: Joe Maloney)

beans on this land. Since then, colonists have found that New Jersey farmlands must be cultivated to feed the big-city multitudes. Today, there are truck farms from the mountains in the north to the sandy plains in the south.

New Jersey has three major farming belts, differentiated by topographical shifts. In the hilly north, there is dairy farming. Poultry and hogs are raised, and grains and other field crops are grown.

The rich, rolling, loamy lands of the midsection of the state are conducive to growing potatoes, spinach, broccoli, asparagus, and—oh, yes—tomatoes. New Jersey's single biggest crop—200,000 tons worth $20 million annually—the tomato has long been closely identified with the state. In the early nineteenth century, superstitions insisted that the "love apple" was a poison and/or an aphrodisiac. But New Jersey judge and civic hero Robert Gibbon Johnson maintained, as did Thomas Jefferson, that tomato cultivation was an idea whose time had come. To prove his point, Judge Johnson consumed an entire bushel of tomatoes at one sitting. Despite the fact that he survived and kept his hormones under control, the crowd remained dubious. And the tomato did not insinuate itself comfortably into the agricultural and culinary life of New Jersey until much later in the century.

The third farming belt is in South Jersey, where the dominant agricul-

Watery wildlands are especially treasured in South Jersey. Left: A quiet backwater in the Pine Barrens, where the soil minerals give the pellucid water a soft feel. (Runk/Schoenberger/Grant Heilman Photography) Above: A gorgeous salt marsh, where the land meets the ocean in Cumberland County. (Anne Ross)

tural products are fruit—from orchards, like peaches and apples; and from bushes, like blueberries, cranberries, and strawberries.

In 1797, Charles Newbold of Burlington County invented the cast-iron plow, only one of many agricultural innovations developed in the state. New Jersey has its own breed of tomato, the Jersey Tomato, and its own hog, the Jersey Red. Giant strawberries have been hybridized, and the little red berries have been inflated up to fifteen to the pound. Though many would argue that these and other hybrids lose some taste on the way to gigantism, quality has always been superseded by quantity in business. And agriculture is nothing if not a business.

Look at the cranberry harvest. For centuries, the humble cranberry was an acquired, local taste. Indians used it medicinally and, because of its acid-sugar balance, as a preservative for some meats. In the Pine Barrens, where the low, straggly bushes thrive in the sandy soil, the berry harvest

has been an important source of income for nearly a century. In the past, teams of laborers would descend on the bogs every autumn, culling the berries with wooden scoop-rakes. But in the 1960s, the wet-harvesting method was introduced. Now, in September, the bogs are flooded, and men pushing water pickers (which look like giant old-fashioned lawn-mowers) wade in, their machines gently knocking the ripe cranberries from the bushes. This method is more efficient but also requires a bigger capital investment—in land and machines—to pay off. Thus with this new efficiency has come a narrowing of the field. Where once hundreds of individual landowners could make a small living from their cranberries, now, with large-scale techniques, most cannot compete—and there are only about 50 producers left in the state.

Small farmers everywhere face hard times, due to a wide variety of complex economic problems. In 1925, New Jersey had approximately

New Jersey may well be the homeland of the American lawn. Here, two different styles of living with nature in the northern suburbs. Opposite: A happy tangle of deciduous trees over the neighbor's fence. Above: An elaborately groomed, almost Japanese, approach to the notion of the backyard. (Both: Joe Maloney)

Overleaf: A riot of spring flowers cultivated at an arboretum in Summit. (Anne Ross)

30,000 mid-size family farms; now, there are fewer than 9,000, and many of these are failing. This is a trend that holds throughout the northeastern United States, but in New Jersey farmers have the added incentive of valuable acreage—which usually goes to condo development—to sell out and leave the land.

An overview of New Jersey farming would be incomplete without mention of the Seabrook family. What started in the late nineteenth century as 57 acres of south-central farmland accumulated in the hands of successive Seabrooks to 6,000 cultivated acres of peas, beans, and spinach—and the agricultural empire known as Seabrook Farms. Key to the Seabrooks' success was their innovative use of frozen-food packaging. (Clarence Birdseye was in fact employed by Seabrook Farms before he left and joined General Foods as a competitor.) Seabrook Farms was sold during the 1960s. Due primarily to the high cost of labor and the long northern winters, the new owners left and relocated on the West Coast. Most recently, however, a new generation of Seabrooks has opened up a large new food-processing plant in South Jersey. The new company, called Seabrook Brothers and Sons, has also revived some acreage for planting, and it employs local farmers in a sort of enlightened version of tenant farming.

Other major food processors in the state are Campbell's Soup, Snow's, Ocean Spray (cranberries), and Progresso (tomatoes). New Jersey boosters maintain that the farmers and the processors need to work hand in hand in the state and that with such food-processing plants located in New Jersey cities, even urban workers can be employed in agribusiness.

The harvesting of fish and shellfish along the shore is another aspect of Jersey food production. A $500 million industry now, this is expanding, with especially plentiful squid and mackerel catches.

Meanwhile, hope for the small farmer has been extended recently, in the form of metropolitan green markets. New York, Philadelphia, Wilmington, and cities throughout New Jersey, have regular green markets; and their popularity is growing. In the city, selling right off the truck at low prices, a small New Jersey farmer can profit from his vegetables, fruit, garden plants and shrubs, home-smoked meats, honey from his hives, and baked goods from his kitchen.

Bruce Springsteen tossed off a joke at his Meadowlands concerts to the effect that the Garden of Eden had not been in Mesopotamia but "was actually located 10 miles south of Jersey City, just off the New Jersey Turnpike—and that's why they call this the Garden State!" It would be hard to miss the bitter affection implicit in that joke, the pride of place coupled with the rage of loss. Of course, Western man has expelled himself from Eden again and again, bulldozing and paving and overpopulating and poisoning the land. Ten miles south of Jersey City is now mostly an embalming swamp for dead cars, a desolate landscape marked by the eerie intermittent blaze of fire from the petroleum refineries. Technically, this entire region is a salt marsh, hundreds of square miles of twisting tributar-

The Garden State feeds much of the Northeast. Opposite: A bird's-eye view of a family farm in Sussex County. (Bob Krist) Above: Bush green beans thrive in the rich soil of the center of the state. (Left: John Colwell/Grant Heilman Photography; Right: Grant Heilman/Grant Heilman Photography)

Above: Corn shocks in Foster Field preserve the continuity of rural life since the days of the first settlers. (E. R. Degginger)
Right: A friendly meeting in the Pine Barrens. (Bob Krist)

ies and mucky little islands. Once upon a time it was a beautiful wetlands habitat for all manner of mammals, reptiles and birds, a sweeping flat of emerald green.

But as a state, New Jersey is trying harder. Because of its small size, incredible density of population, and high degree of industrialization, New Jersey has had to face up to environmental issues sooner than nearly any other state in the Union. The results, in terms of wilderness preservation, have been encouraging; in any case, the rate of destruction has been retarded.

All along the Delaware River, that snakelike boundary that separates New Jersey from Pennsylvania and Delaware, the landscape is intensely picturesque. From High Point (the highest spot in the state, at 1,805 feet above sea level) in High Point State Park, one can observe the river below, flowing in a deep trough that cuts through the Kittatinny Ridge of the Appalachian Mountains. The trough cuts deepest a little further downstream, on a three-mile stretch of the river called the Delaware Water Gap. The dramatic rise of mountains on both sides, and the lovely islands in midstream, made this a favorite vista for the landscape painter George Inness—as well as a perennially popular tourist site. Water Gap National Park and nearby Worthington State Forest are densely covered with a range of deciduous trees and with shaggy hemlock, spruce, cedar, and Scotch pine.

Many of New Jersey's smaller rivers also have their scenic attractions, and canoeing is encouraged. The Paulins Kill and the Musconetcong River both rush through the Kittatinnies to join the Delaware. The Batsto,

Mullica, Wading, and Oswego rivers—like the Maurice River and the Great Egg Harbor River—traverse the wilds of the Pine Barrens. In the backwaters of Toms River and the Metedeconk River, smugglers have holed up since Revolutionary times. Although man-made, the canal that joins the Raritan and Delaware rivers (and which, in its heyday, carried more tonnage than the Erie Canal) is now empty of commercial traffic. Its calm sixty-mile length is an acclaimed beauty spot for paddling tourists and ornithologists.

Although much of New Jersey's coastline has been given over forever to commercial and residential development, a number of parks and wildlife areas preserve some of the shore's original splendor. Sandy Hook, Barnegat, and Brigantine wildlife refuges host egrets, herons, woodcock, catbirds, thrashers, and mockingbirds, along with muskrats, rabbits, snakes, wildflowers, and trees. One of the more beguiling features of the New Jersey shore is the Marine Mammal Stranding Center in Brigantine, just north of Atlantic City. With minimal financing, this center rescues and nurses wayward whales, seals, dolphins, porpoises, and turtles. Most of the animals needing help get stranded while they are migrating along New Jersey's coast and are not in fact permanent residents of the state—which is the main reason the center has trouble getting help from state-based funding sources.

But of all the spectacular and exotic natural areas in the state, none comes close in size or significance to the Pine Barrens. About a thousand square miles of the original region are still wild lands—principally those protected by the Lebanon State Forest and the Wharton State Forest. The Pine Barrens is geologically unique; in the Miocene Epoch, some 2 million years ago, it was an island, roughly eighty miles long and thirty miles wide. Several hundred thousand years were to pass before the rest of New Jersey rose up from the sea to join it. In the seventeenth and eighteenth centuries, when European colonists first came to the pine forest, they found its sandy soil discouraged farming; and so they called it, somewhat disparagingly, the Pine Barrens. Over the centuries, it has been home to outcasts (Hessians, Tories, blacks, and Indians) and outlaws (smugglers, pirates, and worse) who have intermarried with the basic Anglo-Saxon population that dominates the Appalachian region. Residents of the Pines are called, by themselves as well as by outsiders, "Pineys." Of late, New Jersey's tourism board has tried to rename the Pine Barrens as the more banal "Pinelands," inhabited by "Pinelanders," but one trusts that such euphemisms are doomed to failure.

In the eighteenth and nineteenth centuries, the bog iron that the eons had seen fit to deposit in the area was mined, and large populations settled

A hymn to the vanishing family farm: A boy, his goat, and his cat. (Tom Herde)

A unique natural habitat, the Pine Barrens—the land of sandy soil, quiet rivers, bog iron, pines, and "Pineys"—has a geological history eons old and a human history that dates back several thousand years. The original inhabitants, the Lenni-Lenape Indians, have vanished as a culture, though their bloodlines can still be traced among the Pineys. Preserving the region has become an important goal for the state. (All: Mick Hales)

Overleaf: On such still streams as this, much of the Pine Barrens can be visited by canoe. (Mick Hales)

AT WORK

Despite the near presence of those concentrated job markets, New York and Philadelphia, most of New Jersey's laboring men and women do not leave the state to earn their daily bread. Thousands of manufacturing and retail concerns flourish in New Jersey, and many well-known companies have chosen to establish corporate headquarters here. In recent years, the tug of war with New York City for tenant corporations has led to some expedient modification of tax laws on both sides—and though it cannot be denied that New York still leads the field, New Jersey has made some gains. The building of the waterfront—especially Newport City and Harborside in Jersey City—can also provide "back-office" and data-center sites for New York City companies such as Bankers Trust Company.

How the state stacks up: Blueberries, like cranberries, are a leading crop in South Jersey; orange juice migrates north from Florida, pausing in a depot near Harrison. (Opposite: Bob Krist; Left: Ray Mortenson)

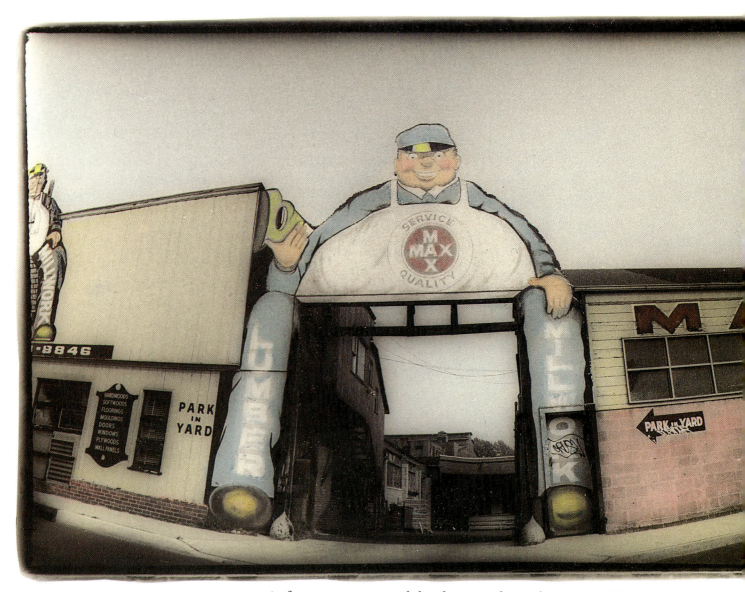

As for corporations with headquarters here: there are AT&T and A&P, Squibb pharmaceuticals and Union Camp paper bags, Coca-Cola and Johnson & Johnson, Nissan and Mercedes-Benz, Campbell's Soup and Lenox china to serve it in, Benjamin Moore paint and Allied Chemicals paint remover—and Nabisco, Volvo, Toyota. New Jersey is home to a true cross-section of international commerce; and while drugs, food, chemicals, and cars dominate here, as in the lives of all Americans, they do so along with the likes of Hartz Mountain pet products, Port-O-San toilets, and Prentice-Hall publishers.

While the nation's unemployment rate hovers around 7 percent at this writing, New Jersey does somewhat better, with only 4.4 percent unemployed. However, the cities—Newark with 11 percent, Camden with 12.6 percent—look about as bad as cities throughout the U.S. For those who take a dim view of the current litigation explosion, New Jersey's

25,500 lawyers may seem a bit dispiriting—but it's all a part of a statewide shift from a predominantly manufacturing work force to one given over largely to white-collar and service jobs—89 percent of all jobs in the state, in fact.

With the shifting work-force profile may come some diminution of one of New Jersey's principal features: its smells. Lawyers usually reek only of such upwardly mobile aromas as aftershave and garlic from fancy French lunches. Think of the heavy odor of Maxwell House coffee that hovers like a loving mother over Hoboken, or that sulfur smell from the Mobil and other petroleum refineries along the Bayonne-Elizabeth stretch of the Turnpike. Along the south shore, you can still get that breathtaking, fresh salty stink of the catch from the fishing fleets—and throughout the state, the springtime essence of cow can be savored when manure is spread on the farm fields. The twentieth century likes to turn up its nose at smells,

but even lawyers do, occasionally—despite the efforts of a hundred different products—sweat.

New Jersey is spiritual homeland to a quintessentially American institution: the industrial park. Like temples of a righteous Modernist faith, these one- and two-story glass and cement complexes, set on artificially rolling landscapes, with curving driveways and camouflaged parking lots, bring the gospel of research technology to the hinterlands of Morris Plains, Totowa, and Vineland. (The industrial park, of course, shares its crisp golf-course looks with suburban drive-in banks, public schools, and even churches.)

Route 1 between New Brunswick and Princeton has grown thick with industrial parks. Small, thriving high-tech concerns are run by the "new pioneers" of industry. These young entrepreneurs, who will risk everything for a new software package, are turning this region into the Silicon Valley of the East.

More traditionally-minded research and business wizards might well go to work for the grandfather of them all, Bell Labs in Murray Hill and in Holmdel. It was for their work at the Holmdel labs that a pair of scientists won the Nobel Prize for Physics in 1978, when they recorded the lingering echo of the original Big Bang.

Where does all this talent come from? Much of it comes straight from the halls of New Jersey's colleges and universities—including the Stevens Institute of Technology in Hoboken and Rutgers, the State University of New Jersey, located on the Raritan River in New Brunswick, which has a famed College of Engineering. Founded in 1766, Rutgers is integral to the educational life of the state, as it is one of the principal state colleges for training public school teachers.

New Jersey's public school system evolved from the nineteenth-century "free school" movement, of which Clara Barton (later the founder of the American Red Cross) was an early champion. The free schools were set up

Mercedes-Benz has found a sleek home in Montvale, where it produces parts in a surreal fluorescent setting. Toyota, Nissan, and Volvo also have their American headquarters in the state. (Both: Wolfgang Hoyt/ESTO)

as a means to educate the children of the poor, whose parents could not pay for private tuition. At first, these schools were subsidized by charity. Later, the state took an active interest and united them under one public system, supplementing local funds with government monies. Today, the system boasts a strong track record in both academic and vocational training.

Among the state's private secondary schools, one of the most renowned is Lawrenceville Academy for boys. Lawrenceville—with its small brick buildings and its manicured lawns—is the perfect adolescent counterpart to its big brother down the road: Princeton.

In 1746, Princeton was the fifth college in the colonies. Established by the Presbyterians, it remains an emblem of ultra-conservatism even within the Ivy League and retains some upper-crust airs—with its exclusive dining clubs, high cost, and predominantly WASP confidence in its own traditions.

Nassau Hall, the stately building that signifies the entire university to many, in fact once housed all its activities. In June 1783, the Continental Congress, meeting in Philadelphia, found itself threatened by rioting soldiers who had yet to receive their back pay from service in the Revolution. Fearing bodily harm, the Congressmen adjourned and, at the invitation of Princeton's president, reconvened in Nassau Hall, from which the U.S. government officially operated until November. How fitting that Princeton should have provided, then as now, a haven from the angry mob.

Many college-age men and women these days spend their time working in New Jersey for a federal employer: the military. Picatinny Arsenal, in Dover, has been a storage and manufacturing center since the Revolution. In the Second World War, Picatinny was the country's leading manufacturer of large-scale munitions, and in 1950, the arsenal had the dubious distinction of producing the first nuclear shell to be used in artillery weapons. Today, Picatinny remains one of the largest employers in Morris County.

In the otherwise peaceful hamlet of Wrightstown, Fort Dix, one of the nation's major permanent army installations, hunkers down next to McGuire Air Force Base. Thousands of young men and women are trained on Fort Dix's fifty square miles. No wonder it boasts that it is "the home of the ultimate weapon—the American soldier." Dix and McGuire share the Walson Army Hospital facilities.

The military is a strong presence and a major employer in the state. Here, recruits line up for morning exercises at Fort Dix. Established as an army base during the First World War, the facility covers more than 50 square miles. (Mark R. Jenkinson)

Nearby is Lakehurst Naval Air Engineering Center, which of late has gone a long way toward furthering its reputation as a disaster area. (The *Hindenburg* famously failed to dock properly there in 1937 and, even more famously, blew up.) Lakehurst has recently been charged with dumping toxic wastes into the local water supply. A statewide controversy has developed, as local environmentalists and the federal Environmental Protection Agency charge that Lakehurst may have irretrievably poisoned the Pine Barrens aquifer. Since the military is not legally subject to the EPA's rulings, information is hard to come by, and legal action—so far—next to impossible.

Meanwhile, there remain many fields of employment in which nature is the boss. New Jersey's farmers, fishermen, and foresters may be statistically small groups, but their labors have a significance far beyond the reach of mere numbers.

The new volunteer army shows itself to be composed of all shapes and sizes, above. At Fort Dix, as well as at Lakehurst and McGuire Air Force bases, recruits learn as they drill, are cheered on as they learn (far left) and learn as they launder (near left). (All: Mark R. Jenkinson)

Above: A hog—perhaps one of the state's own Jersey Red variety—is butchered on a small family farm in northwestern Sussex County. (Larry Fink)
Opposite: Yet another of Flemington Fur's satisfied customers. (George Tice)

AT WORK • 97

The state's wide variety of natural and man-made settings has long made it a favorite of filmmakers. Thousands of movies have been shot in New Jersey, from the first decades of the twentieth century, when the industry was headquartered in Fort Lee, to the present day. Some scenes of Annie were shot in Newark in 1980. (Both: Mitch Epstein)

The slogan on this bridge (which spans the Delaware River between Trenton and Morrisville, Pennsylvania) could be read as either a boast or a complaint. The line was hatched in 1910 by a man named Roy Heath, and was chosen the winner over 1,477 other entries in a Chamber of Commerce-sponsored contest. (Jan Staller)

The Santore family of Millington has been involved in the manufacture and deployment of Fourth of July fireworks for a very long time, almost since patriarch August Santore immigrated to New Jersey in 1890. Today, fireworks are not just for the Fourth anymore, and the third-generation business is regarded as one of the premier fireworks makers in the world. The company offers some 120 styles of shells for an incredible variety of sound and light effects, and it puts on some 250 shows a year. Top: Dan LaSasso and Chester Turiano with drying racks. Above: Other family members prepare a launch site. (All: Peter Ralston)

Overleaf: Every fall, the cranberry bogs of the Pine Barrens are flooded to facilitate the harvesting of the berries, one of the state's major crops. (E. R. Degginger)

THE SHORE

The words "Jersey" and "shore" have been linked for a very long time. The state was famous for its beaches before Miami had a name, before Long Island was known for anything but potatoes. New Jersey's wide-open coastline, 127 miles of it, accessible to New York City and Philadelphia, has been a resort area since the beginning of the nineteenth century. Long Branch was established as a bathing spa by 1819, and Atlantic City and Cape May followed not long after.

It is not hard to see why this popularity was achieved so early. The Jersey shore has an astonishing variety of beaches, all of them combining friendly

Opposite: Cape May, New Jersey's land's end. (Jan Staller) Left: The harmony of boat, water, and shore. (George Tice)

stretches of land with a vigorous pounding surf. The state has, in fact, a double shore; it possesses a string of outer islands, running most of the way down the coast, which front on the ocean and protect the inland waterway. This linked collection of inlets, bays, and canals, officially called the Intracoastal Waterway, runs from Manasquan to the far end of the Cape May Canal, totaling 116 miles within the state, and eventually goes all the way to Florida. The waterway effectively divides the outer shore, the playground, from the inner one, the working coast.

The Jersey shore is usually said to begin around Keyport, an old-time fishing town high up on the state's hip, just below Perth Amboy. Between there and Cape May, at the state's southern tip, can be found a bewildering array of communities and cultures. For years, the northern beaches were in grave danger from the pollution of New York Bay, but recent efforts, centering around the reclamation of Sandy Hook as a nature preserve, have done much to revive the area. The bay towns—Keyport, Keansburg, Highlands, and Atlantic Highlands—are no longer bathing resorts, but they still afford a considerable amount of recreational fishing. This part of the shore is now densely built up, but a long history still resounds, with associations from the Revolutionary War to the rum-running days of Prohibition. Sandy Hook juts up from the hip, a long sliver with a wildlife sanctuary and a military installation, topped off by the Sandy Hook Light. Just below the Hook the bathing beaches begin. Sea Bright is divided from the mainland by the Navesink and Shrewsbury rivers, and it thus possesses much of the same "strip" quality as the island towns farther south. Sea Bright also begins the parade of motels, condos, beach clubs, singles bars, and cabana tracts that extend southward. It is a loud and public town and presumes to set the tone for the following hundred miles. This is a bit misleading, since the next town, Monmouth Beach, is rather suburban and recessive, albeit dominated by several enormous condominium slabs that look as though they might have flown up from Hollywood, Florida.

Long Branch is the dowager of the coast. In the nineteenth century and into the twentieth, it was the resort of presidents and powerbrokers, of Lillian Russell and Diamond Jim Brady. Apparently bathing on its beach was at first segregated by sex; later it became illegal for women to walk into the surf unescorted. Today, Long Branch is a large if somewhat scattered town that seems to lack any center except for its boardwalk amusement area. The prosperous and very private community of Deal follows. The first things the traveler notices are its unusual Art Nouveau lampposts, which bend in toward the street like so many vegetable stalks. Deal, composed of sumptuous white houses dating from the 1890s-1920s, could not contrast more vividly with its neighbor, Asbury Park.

Lucy the Elephant, of Margate City, is one of the state's oldest and most respected citizens. She weighs 90 tons and is 6 stories tall, 38 feet long, and 80 feet in circumference. She is made of tin-covered wood and was built about a hundred years ago by a Philadelphia real estate man named James V. Lafferty, who hoped to turn her into an office building and planned to build dozens of other such structures in the shape of birds, fish, and mammals. Lucy has survived several major hurricanes, has been sold and moved, and finally has been declared a national landmark. (New Jersey Division of Travel & Tourism)

Asbury Park is a very poor town clustered around a dilapidated board-walk with imposing, if decayed, Victorian pleasure palaces. It is a smaller version of what Atlantic City was like before gambling was legalized, but Asbury Park has found no takers. It has been passed up by one development company after another, possibly on account of its limited size. Asbury Park's favorite son is Bruce Springsteen, who has called it "Newark-by-the-Sea." He got his start at the Stone Pony, which stands directly opposite the miniature golf course, and he occasionally will duck in to play a surprise set there. He has come to personify New Jersey for a great many people, which is fine. It has also led to some interesting ironies. In 1980, his "Born to Run" was named the state's "unofficial rock anthem" by the State Legislature, an unusual fate for a song celebrating the urgency of getting out of town. In any case, Bruce now lives in nearby Rumson and plays local benefits, not at all shirking his role as a symbol of the state.

Keeping Asbury Park small are its neighbors, the aforementioned Deal to the north, and the former holy city of Ocean Grove to the south. From 1869 until 1980 Ocean Grove closed its gates between midnight Saturday and midnight Sunday and forbade driving, boating, swimming, and all

other commercial activities during those hours. It was a theocracy administered by the Methodist Church. Its blue laws have been repealed as unconstitutional, and profane parties have been slowly moving in. Nevertheless, this Jerusalem-by-the-Sea retains much of its character. At night it looks across the stream at the gaudy, illuminated Sodom that is Asbury Park with a dark eye. During the day its great gingerbread-gothic hotels face the sea all in white like so many pilgrim souls. Infidels have lately begun painting some of them in pastel colors, but fortunately the change is not much in evidence yet. During the summer the devout still flock to Ocean Grove from around the country, some dwelling in tents on platforms, all their settlements radiating outward from the Auditorium. This structure, the temple of the town, was built, like Solomon's temple, without the use of nails. Before heathen influences swamp the town, it remains briefly possible to walk through on a Sunday evening and hear nothing but the roar of the surf.

The Methodist sanctuary is succeeded by the largely Jewish Bradley Beach, the first of a string of placid family resorts. There is Avon-by-the-Sea, once known as a center of adult education; Belmar, with its boat basin;

The shore affords a rich variety of the pleasures of the flesh. Opposite: Our man finds himself treated like a pasha in his perfumed garden, surrounded by neo-mirage architecture. Actually, he's getting a little of the Atlantic City sun and reading a biography of Winston Churchill. (William Suttle) Above: Two girls on the Asbury Park boardwalk dare the passerby to say anything at all. (Joe Maloney)

Spring Lake, which features a Catholic church that looks like a miniature of St. Peter's in Rome, as well as two extraordinary turn-of-the-century hotels, the Warren and the Essex and Sussex. There are the working-class resorts of Sea Girt and Manasquan, and boating towns like Point Pleasant, Bay Head, and Mantoloking. Around this point a peninsula begins to stretch down through Normandy Beach and Lavallette to Seaside Heights. Seaside Heights possesses the largest amusement frontage in the area, with a full-scale carousel and ferris wheel, as well as the usual cotton-candy dispensaries and shooting galleries.

Just to the south of Seaside Heights lies the lovely Island Beach State Park—not actually situated on an island, but running to the end of the peninsula. For most of its length, the park is a slender bulwark of dunes protecting Barnegat Bay, with bits of vegetation preserving the original character of the coastal islands. "Old Barney," the Barnegat Lighthouse, sits on the northern tip of Long Beach Island, just across from the peninsula's southernmost point. A lighthouse was originally erected on this spot in 1834, and the present structure dates back to 1858. It has not functioned since 1943, but it remains a sentimental favorite landmark and the focus of numerous local legends and ghost stories. (Captain Kidd is only one of several pirates supposed to have buried treasure on the island.) The island itself is a strip of subtly various beach towns—with colorful names like Loveladies, Ship Bottom, and Surf City—which roar in the summer and sleep through the rest of the year.

South of the island is Little Egg Inlet, leading to the Great Bay. Nowadays the region is mostly known for its wildlife, protected under a variety of auspices—the Brigantine National Wildlife Refuge and the Great Bay and Absecon Wildlife Management Areas—whose jurisdiction covers a relatively wide area of marshland and islands all the way down to Atlantic City. What all this obscures is the region's extraordinary past. Few people realize that Tuckerton, tucked sleepily into Little Egg Harbor, was a port of major importance in the eighteenth century, ranking with New York, Philadelphia, and Charleston. Its prominence was almost entirely dependent on the bog iron industry in the Pine Barrens. When that enterprise faded, so did Tuckerton.

South of the inlet, the relatively isolated town of Brigantine sits on its own island at the end of a road. Below it stands the Absecon Lighthouse,

This imposing Italianate stucco villa in Deal has succeeded in remaking the sun and the sea into its own image of airbrushed perfection. (Mark Stern)

Above: When Atlantic City changed its face, it jettisoned a great deal of dross and much that was decidedly not dross. For example, the Marlborough-Blenheim Hotel, a vision of Moorish stateliness, was dynamited in 1979. (All: John Margolies/ESTO) Opposite: A view of the Atlantic as a giant bathtub, with tiny toy boats merrily bobbing on long, graceful waves. (Grant Heilman/ Grant Heilman Photography)

This couple's souvenir album will soon be graced by a casual shot taken in front of a lineup of Atlantic City's most jellyfishlike tents. (William Suttle)

Overleaf: The typical geometry of the shore's weatherbeaten wooden architecture. (Henri Cartier-Bresson/MAGNUM)

and below that, Atlantic City. A decade ago, the city was nearly a ghost town, full of crumbling architectural gems, with a moldering boardwalk and a moribund collection of carny stands. Today it is Babylon. The casino industry, having razed some of the city's outstanding landmarks, employs 40,535 people, more than the city's total population, and pays 62.4 percent of the city's property taxes. Nevertheless, the inner city is still very poor. Only time will tell whether the poor will be pushed out of Atlantic City or whether they will be absorbed by it. The Monopoly-board streets continue into Ventnor and Margate City, two charming and prosperous suburbs relatively unaffected by the decay of their hub, but profiting from its revival. The latter town boasts Lucy the Elephant, the only completed specimen of a whole bestiary of buildings planned in the 1880s.

From Brigantine to Cape May, the outer islands are all linked together by toll bridges. South of Margate City and the smaller town of Longport is Great Egg Harbor Inlet, below which is Ocean City, another once-holy city, founded by Methodists in 1879, but profane since the 1950s. The road then passes through the Marmora Wildlife Management Area, through the bungalow colonies of Sea Isle City and Townsends Inlet, through Avalon with its high dunes, and through Stone Harbor, with its bird sanctuary for herons, egrets, ibises.

Then come the Wildwoods. The island of that name is a cluster of towns bearing names with variations on it—North Wildwood, Wildwood City, Wildwood Crest. These names evidently derived from the formerly pristine and abundant aspect of the vegetation, even including substantial tree growth, a rarity on the islands. Now the island is mostly barren of plant life but thick with single-story dwellings. Wildwood City has a raucous boardwalk with all the usual attractions—shooting galleries, palm readers, cotton candy, and skilo ball stands—as well as an extraordinary collection of motels. These motels are uniformly 1950s Moderne in style, and their names—Lido, Versailles, Breakers, Sands—are redolent of Las Vegas and Miami Beach. The effect is like a miniature of those cities, capitals of sin where nothing is all that sinful.

The final, southernmost bridge leads over an inlet linked to the Cape May Canal. Cape May proper might as well be on an island. Although it is technically part of the mainland, it is surrounded entirely by water. The atmosphere here is markedly different as well. The old Victorian hotels clustered around the town's center have been meticulously renovated, and they attract an affluent clientele. The tone is decorous and civilized. It is a town conscious of its position; it is the state's remotest spot, which in a small state is a major distinction. At the tip is the last lighthouse, which, on a clear day, offers a rare view of Delaware.

Cape May, at the state's southern tip, is the last holdout of shore aristocracy. It was already a noted resort at the beginning of the nineteenth century, and drew its share of presidents and celebrities. Today it preserves a quaint charm with its tea shops, its gingerbread Victoriana, its dog shows, and its bicyclists. (Both: Bob Krist)

The point itself, Cape May Light, gives a heady feeling of remoteness that is not readily found elsewhere in the state. These two photos suggest the eerie feeling brought on by sunset, solitude, and a sea breeze. (Both: Jan Staller)

Overleaf: Tailgate parties and clambakes bring generations together on the beach, always a festive setting. (Bob Krist)

AT PLAY

New Jersey's longstanding reputation as a resort does not come only from its seacoast. As an amusement spot, it has purveyed both the bucolic and the worldly. The former attribute derives from its diverse landscape—its hills, lakes, fields, and streams—set conveniently close to cities and ports. The latter quality began to be deliberately pursued and manufactured in the early nineteenth century, when Hoboken's Castle Stevens, with its beer gardens and dance halls, first flourished as a precursor of Coney Island.

Ever since, New Jersey has hosted a long line of carnivals and amusement parks. The best known of these was probably the late, lamented Palisades Park, immortalized by Freddy "Boom-Boom" Cannon's 1960 hit

A couple of linebackers in Giants Stadium hastily drink from their helmets after a rough workout; fiddling Pineys get down on a Saturday night. (Opposite: Tom Herde; Left: Bob Krist)

The Asbury Park carousel is an antique within an antique. The city's
amusement palace, built in a high Victorian seaside mode, survives, albeit
in a relatively dilapidated form. If the visitor squints, temporarily blurring
the view of video games and Springsteen T-shirts, the past comes to life.
(Both: Len Jenshel)

song. Palisades Park was a colossal attraction standing on the cliffs directly across the Hudson River from Manhattan and amusing several generations of metropolitan youth. Midways continue to dot the landscape. There are survivors of an earlier era, such as the Clementon River Park, near Camden, and the charming Bertrand Island Park on Lake Hopatcong, with its prewar ambience. Elsewhere are the late-model extravaganzas, Action Park, in Vernon Valley, and Six Flags Great Adventure, in Jackson, which boast the most advanced refinements of amusement technologies.

Fun-seekers more advanced in years and unburdened by small children are apt to find the appropriate thrills at the gaming tables of the Atlantic City casinos. Atlantic City has been known for a century as a center of jollity, but it is only within the last decade that gambling has been legalized. The vast Moorish hotels and the arcade complexes of the Steel and Million Dollar piers finally came down after crumbling for decades; the carousels were sold and the last diving horses retired. In their place went up multimillion-dollar casino-hotel packages, many of them spun off from Las

Princeton's crew team strokes across Lake Carnegie at an early morning workout. The lake is actually a wide spot in the Millstone River made wider by damming. The project was financed by Andrew Carnegie, who felt it imperative that such an august institution should have a major body of water at hand. (Michael A. Smith)

Vegas models, such as Tropicana, the Golden Nugget, the Sands, and Caesar's. Harrah's has two casino hotels, as does Trump, Inc., while Playboy, Bally's, Resorts International, and Del Webb's own one each, with more hotels opening every year. The casinos have not merely revitalized Atlantic City, they have altered the world's impression of the state, thereby affecting roads, housing, and jobs in South Jersey to a degree that would have seemed incredible a decade ago. The atmosphere in the casinos is strangely concentrated and intense, suggesting a sense almost of worship rather than abandon. The croupiers and change-makers officiate, the players attempt to bend chance with mental force, the onlookers kibitz and echo and chant the chorus. The carpets are deep, the lighting not too bright. Money talks.

Outside, the highways are dense with roadhouses. The basic model of the bar-with-music has held steady since at least the repeal of Prohibition (before which music was not so important a draw), styles changing every few years. In New Jersey one could tour from one roadhouse to another for

weeks, tracing the history of popular music over the last thirty years. There are doo-wop joints in Paramus and Cherry Hill, late-hippie country-rock beer halls in Stirling and Dover, jacket-and-tie discotheques in the Oranges, in Mount Holly, in Bergenfield. There is heavy metal in Paramus, new wave in Hoboken, salsa and charanga in Union City. Most of these places are accessible for a minimal cover charge and the price of a drink. The affinity groups are loose and tend to accommodate outsiders, whatever reserve there is dissolving into fellowship sometime during the second set or third drink.

Very few of these places are located in towns. They tend instead to be on highways of the older "strip" type, and some are even in shopping malls. In New Jersey roads are less likely to link hubs with one another than to be hubs themselves. A casual observer might be led to think that New Jersey's most widespread leisure activity is parking. A Martian might find it especially amusing to watch New Jerseyans drive long distances and exert further time and energy in parking, solely for the privilege of watching strange caricatures of automobiles race down a quarter-mile track in three

Above: The Stone Pony, the Asbury Park juke joint associated with the rise of Bruce Springsteen. Right: The Stone Pony seen from across the boardwalk's miniature golf course, a particularly festive specimen bedecked with very artificial palms. (Both: Joe Maloney)

Pint-sized schussers are taught the rudiments of the triumphant wave by an instructor on the Vernon Valley slopes. (New Jersey Division of Travel & Tourism)

seconds. In New Jersey, speed is held as an aesthetic ideal. Other societies that prize velocity might cite the boredom of endless flat ribbons of highway as the reason. In New Jersey the fascination is much purer. Residents do not need to drive thirty miles to the grocery store, as they do in Montana, but they may choose to do so for the sheer love of the road. Therefore, it is not too surprising that when a New Jerseyan feels the need for inspiration, he might repair to the Old Bridge or Englishtown Raceway Parks or to the Atco Raceway. There he watches ammonia-burning dragsters immolating themselves in a race that is over almost before it has begun, or pickup trucks with bulldozer tires climbing over each other in lakes of mud as the audience covers itself with plastic sheets, or simply souped-up cars endlessly rounding a track the size of the high-school parking lot.

Horse racing, although slower, also has immense appeal in the state. Devotees flock to the Freehold and Monmouth Park racecourses, to the Atlantic City Raceway, to Garden State Park in Cherry Hill, and to the Meadowlands Arena. The latter even features winter harness racing under its dome. It features, in fact, a great deal more than that. The Brendan

Byrne Stadium in the Meadowlands Sports and Recreation Complex, to use the place's full title, has been standing on reclaimed land on Route 3 in East Rutherford for less than a decade, and yet it is already home to five top teams—the football Giants and Generals, the soccer-playing Cosmos, the basketball Nets, and the hockey Devils, each of whom is the first major-league professional outfit in its sport to bear "New Jersey" before its name. There is no baseball, at least not yet, which is ironic since baseball was first played in New Jersey. Hoboken's Knickerbocker Giants hosted a New York team on the Elysian Fields in 1846. The state has always had its college teams, of course—notably Rutgers and Princeton in football, Fairleigh Dickinson, Seton Hall, and St. Peter's-Jersey City in basketball. Basketball is of particular importance, inspiring the same kind of ferocious loyalties in New Jersey that football does in Iowa. This, we might venture, is the result of the relative physical scales of the two games. A small state would naturally be more responsive to a sport in which the action tends toward the vertical.

Less formal amusements abound in New Jersey. There are fishing, canoeing, hiking, and camping in the northwestern and south central parts

Five nuns demonstrate a religious devotion to fresh New Jersey shellfish as they line up for deep-fried specialties at this stand in Stone Harbor. (Bob Krist)

Overleaf: A pit bull rises to the occasion. (Joe Maloney)

of the state. There are many golf courses, including some very good ones—like Baltusrol in Summit. There are driving ranges, skeet-shooting ranges, rifle ranges. It is possible to hang-glide, to toboggan, to ride horses. There are some excellent ski slopes in the Ramapo Mountains and in the Watchung Range.

Whatever recreations citizens choose to pursue in the privacy of their own homes can have no shortage in New Jersey, a world capital of bedroom communities. In passing one might note the phenomenon of naturist or nudist colonies. The earlier part of the century saw a number of these established in the state, including the enormous Sunshine Camp in Mays Landing, held to be the "world capital of nudism." It has not survived, but nudism hangs on, albeit with a much lower profile, in enclaves sequestered in the remoter rural areas. These camps share an aura of inaccessibility with certain resorts of the rich and famous, in the hunt country and along the upper Palisades. Speculation is also a popular pastime in New Jersey.

Tourism profits from all of the above, but the New Jerseyan's sheer love of driving has also built up a strong intrastate tourist industry. There is no sightseeing experience quite like that of plying the New Jersey highways, stopping to inspect ten thousand cement birdbaths in Parsippany or ten

Opposite: Colts and fillies tear down the straightaway at Freehold. (R. Mackson/FPG Int'l) Above: This gent is already pondering the pleasures of the après-hunt as he sneaks a smoke between foxes in Basking Ridge. (Larry Fink) Left: An equine beauty luxuriates in a bubble bath—a typical bit of pre-race pampering. (Bob Krist)

The mighty Meadowlands Stadium, with a seating capacity of 77,000, hosts the football Giants and Generals, and the Cosmos soccer team, as well as the Jets. It was authorized in May 1971 and finished five years later, taking up 750 acres of swampland that had once seemed unusable. The Meadowlands complex also contains facilities for basketball, hockey, thoroughbred and harness racing, and major pop concerts. (Jim Dow)

Opposite top: A couple of budding athletes in Camden take a breather. (Joe Maloney) Opposite bottom: Investigating the motion of dinosaurs on a patio deck. (Larry Fink) Above: Some kid has it all—pool, hoop, and trike—in a Westwood backyard. (Joe Maloney)

thousand fur coats in Flemington, to gape at the Flagship on Route 22 or the automobile junkyards in Newark, to linger at shopping malls in Woodbridge or Cherry Hill, to dine at Johnny's Hot Dogs in Buttzville or the Lido Diner in Union. One could go on forever uncovering surprises set out in plain sight along New Jersey's highways.

The more respectable arts are no less rich for the state's many frivolities. Theater thrives at the New Jersey Shakespeare Festival at Drew University in Madison, at the Paper Mill Playhouse in Millburn, at theaters in Andover, in Edison, in Hopewell, in Lawrenceville, in Pemberton, in Phillipsburg, in Rutherford and Somerset. The New Jersey Ballet performs in Millburn, the Garden State Ballet in Newark. The Inner City Company stages theater and dance in Paterson, while nine companies work out of the New Jersey Center of Performing Arts in Somerville. There are music festivals at Fairleigh Dickinson University in Madison and at the exquisitely reconstructed Waterloo Village. Tucked away in the state's northwest corner is the scenic Peter's Valley, a residential community and teaching facility for craftsmen that hosts a festival every July. Everywhere there are arts groups and pottery workshops and amateur theatricals and local string quartets. The New Jersey Symphony regularly tours the state. The McCarter Center in Princeton hosts theatrical and musical ensembles from around the world.

New Jersey, after all, has an artistic legacy far richer than even most of its citizens suspect. The motion picture, for example, was developed by Thomas Edison in West Orange and flourished at the famous Fort Lee film colony, where many major companies had their studios before the mass exodus to Hollywood circa the First World War. New Jersey can boast a legion of native sons and daughters gone to glory, artists as diverse as George Inness and Jack Nicholson, Edmund Wilson and Patti Smith, Dorothy Parker and William Wallace Gilchrist (who composed "America the Beautiful"). And New Jersey has its bards: Walt Whitman, who in his later years came to be associated with the city of Camden, and Dr. William Carlos Williams, of Rutherford, whose epic poem, *Paterson*, which follows the course of the Passaic River in five books, is to New Jersey what *Ulysses* is to Dublin.

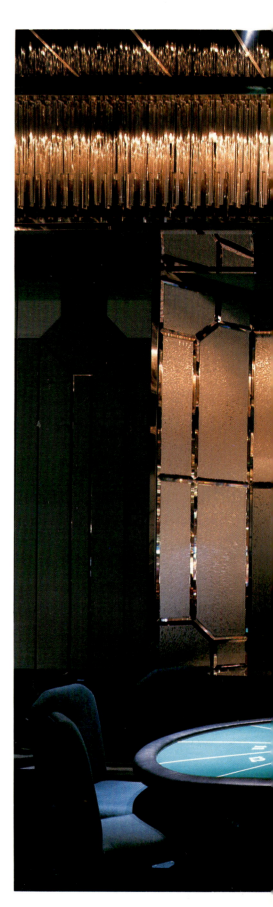

A baccarat table seems to have risen from the ocean floor in the lavish, mirror-encrusted depths of Trump's Castle, Atlantic City. Subdued lighting, deep-pile carpeting, and glittering but not glaring surfaces set a tone of sophisticated cool to control the pitch of gambling fever in the casinos. No one has been heard to complain. (Len Jenshel)

Funny cars burn up the quarter-mile track at Englishtown Raceway Park. The bodies of these freakish vehicles bear a distinct relationship to Detroit products, but there ends any resemblance to the family car. They burn a highly flammable and volatile fuel based on ammonia, possess outlandish suspensions, and stop only with the aid of a parachute. They are absolutely useless for runs to the supermarket. (Joyce Ravid)

Overleaf: Achieving that golden glow at a tanning salon in Fort Lee. (Bob Krist)

THE PAST IN THE PRESENT

There are places in New Jersey, as there are in every state, where one would swear the world was made yesterday. In the center of the Cherry Hill Mall, in the lobby of the Trump Castle in Atlantic City, in the soundproof room at Bell Labs in Murray Hill, there seems to be no past, no intimation of mortality to darken the freshly minted present. A short drive away from any of these, however, the past lurks on tree-shaded roads or on the fringes of cities, sometimes gussied up, sometimes standing dirty and forgotten, but no less real. New Jersey sometimes seems to have gotten its

Opposite: The main waiting room of the Hoboken Conrail station. (Brian Rose) Left: A ghostly trunk line rises from the marsh. (Curt Richter)

history faster than some other places, zipping from colonial agrarian stateliness to high-tech postmodernism in the space of a few months. Everywhere there are reminders that the past was actually much more complicated than that.

New Jersey was originally the home of the Lenni-Lenape Indians, whom the European settlers called Delawares. They were a peace-loving branch of the southern Algonquins, and they had relatively good luck in their commerce with whites, avoiding battles and eventually being bought off. Little remains of Native American culture in the state, most of it centered in the hamlet of Indian Mills in the Pine Barrens, site of a short-lived communal experiment in the late eighteenth century that was the first and the most utopian-minded Indian reservation in the United States.

Giovanni da Verrazano was the first European to see New Jersey, probably anchoring at Sandy Hook and maybe farther north as well on his 1524 expedition. In 1609, Henry Hudson sailed by on his way up the river that was to bear his name. Nine years later, the Dutch established a trading post on the site of Jersey City and continued to build settlements until 1664, when they surrendered New Netherlands to the English. After that, New Jersey—briefly split into two colonies—grew with impressive speed. Newark was settled in 1666, Salem in 1675, Burlington in 1677, Perth Amboy in 1683. The first tavern opened at Woodbridge in 1683, the first pottery at Burlington in 1688. A mail route was established between New York and Philadelphia in 1739. Two important industries, glass and pig iron, were established in 1740 and 1743 respectively. By the time of the Revolution, the state's population was already more than 100,000.

The Revolution looms large in New Jersey, which is not surprising since, as a flat space between two major cities, it was the site of more than a hundred battles, big and small. It is estimated that at least a quarter of George Washington's tenure as commander-in-chief of the Continental Army was spent in New Jersey. This has left no dearth of places in which the Father of his Country is alleged to have slept, including two of his major headquarters, the Dey Mansion in Wayne and the Ford Mansion in Morristown. Jockey Hollow, also in Morristown, was the site of encampments by Washington's army during two severe winters. The first of these (1776-77) began famously at Valley Forge, after which Washington's troops crossed the Delaware and attacked the British Army Barracks at

Two he-men display their tans while showing off the deep polish of their lovingly restored prewar coupe. On such a hot day in Manasquan, it would be hard to say which surface gives off the more intense glow. (Joe Maloney)

Trenton in a daring Christmas Eve raid. These barracks have also been preserved; they are the only surviving example of French and Indian War barracks. The river crossing, besides having been immortalized by Emanuel Leutze's iconic rendition, is commemorated, a bit confusingly, by both the launching and docking sites sprouting towns named Washington Crossing. When the weary Washington finally sat down to compose his "Farewell Address to the Armies," he did so at the Rockingham House in Rocky Hill, which has also been preserved. In all these cases, when the actual pen, or bed, or boot, or sleigh, was unavailable, reasonable approximations have been found.

The eighteenth century, then, survives throughout the state in a succession of handsome Queen Anne, Georgian, and Federal houses, their contents meticulously restored and separated from the crowds by red velvet ropes. There is the Blackledge-Kearny House in Fort Lee, used as a headquarters by Cornwallis, Washington's opposite number; there is the Indian King Tavern in Haddonfield, patronized by Dolley Madison; there is Boxwood Hall in Elizabeth, home of Elias Boudinot, president of the Continental Congress. Even more impressive in some ways are the

Above: This majestic double-barreled Victorian seaside mansion faces the world in Allenhurst. Right: An eighteenth-century Middle Valley fieldstone farmhouse that clearly intends to stick around for a few more centuries, regardless of thunder, lightning, or prevailing winds. (Both: George Tice)

New Jerseyans do not shy away from dazzling ceremonial attire. Above: Princeton alumni, decked out in traditional boaters and blazers, gather in the quad on Class Day. (Bob Krist) Right: A squad of brightly jacketed crooners, attending the barbershop quartet convention in Asbury Park, pause to serenade the boardwalk. (Joe Maloney)

eighteenth-century houses of no particular repute that can be spotted along older and less-traveled roads in rural parts of the state.

If the eighteenth century seems to have produced only a string of patrician country seats, the nineteenth century is quite a different matter. The Industrial Revolution was New Jersey's second upheaval, and it left an even greater mark on the state. Actually, industrial development began long before the invention of the spinning jenny signaled the official beginning of the Factory Age. The Dutch opened the first copper mine in the Kittatinny Mountains in about 1640. Josiah Hornblower imported America's first steam engine in 1753, but the first steam locomotive was built by Hoboken's John Stevens in 1824. The nineteenth century witnessed the most dramatic period of the state's development, from the growth of the bog iron industry in the Pine Barrens (as well as its subsequent decline) to the astonishing string of inventions produced by Thomas Edison at Menlo Park near the century's end.

The Pine Barrens must be the spookiest memorial to industrial archeology in the world. Bustling factory towns of a century and a half ago appear as remote as Troy. In many cases all that is left is a pile of bricks once

Cowboys stretch out and tie on chaps at a rodeo at New Jersey's wild western Woodstown. (Murray Tinkelman)

The eighteenth century awaits the visitor to Waterloo Village, with stocks thoughtfully provided for those who get out of line. (New Jersey Division of Travel & Tourism)

Overleaf: Three bridges cross the Raritan River at Neshansic. (Curt Richter)

constituting a blast furnace, in many more cases there remains nothing but the intersection of a couple of sand roads. A few of these sites have been restored—notably Batsto and Allaire. The restorations are intelligent and scrupulous, although it is a bit hard to see these places as anything but quaint. The wilderness of scrub pine in which they are set does not easily yield up an image of significant industry. Once the traffic had moved on, the very particular local ecology neatly erased its passage.

The planned industrial city of Paterson, first imagined by Alexander Hamilton and built as deliberately as Brasilia, has kept its context, notably the Great Falls, and although its locomotive shops and foundries have been idle for decades, it remains a major city. It is, among other things, crucial to the history of the labor movement as the site of a number of important strikes that helped to raise the minimum wage and shorten the working day. Thomas Edison's laboratories in West Orange (which include materials from the famous Menlo Park site) also convey the significance of the work that he performed there. The tables, desks, and cabinets remain crammed with equipment and documents, with a hectic quality only temporarily stilled, like a factory after hours. After all, it was with that equipment that Edison invented the carbon telephone transmitter in 1876, the phonograph in 1877, the incandescent lamp in 1879, and the motion picture in 1889. Such compulsive creation could not possibly have taken place in tidy surroundings. Also testifying to New Jersey's industrial past is the Speedwell complex at the edge of Morristown, where the telegraph and the transatlantic steamship engine were developed. Then there's the Smithville Mansion in Mount Holly, site of a brief but impressive manufacturing commune of the late nineteenth century. The era's conception of utopia meant hard industrial labor for equal benefits.

The survival of the past in New Jersey means more than buildings, however. It is, for one thing, reflected in place names. There are Indian appellations like Ho-Ho-Kus and Parsippany, plain-spoken rural names like Yellow Frame, Blue Anchor, Ongs Hat, Penny Pot. There are commemorations of immigrant origins: New Egypt, New Lisbon, New Russia—and proud declarations of new societies: Colonia, Ironia, Harmony. There are strange names with obscure histories, and names that seem altogether too obvious—Chrome, for example, or Bivalve, or the hamlet of Miami Beach in Lower Cape May Township. There are at least twelve ways of pronouncing "Newark," just as there are six or seven synonyms for "submarine sandwich" and "pizza pie." Most of all, though, there is a New Jersey attitude—forthright, canny, and alert, a determination not to be passed on the highway of history—that is entirely appropriate to the third state to ratify the Constitution.

Opposite: This Princeton barbershop has groomed many generations of underclassmen, quite a few of whom are pictured in team portraits on the walls. (Both: Michael A. Smith) Above: The signorial elevation of the chairs at the Hoboken train station's shoeshine stand. (Jan Staller)

Left: A bicentennial reenactment of the Battle of Princeton. In early January 1777, George Washington, having crossed from Valley Forge and attacked Trenton, continued his thrust by attacking the redcoats head-quartered in Princeton. The battle was a considerable victory, resulting in numerous British casualties. For their part, the colonists lost General Hugh Mercer, after whom Mercer County is named. (Bob Krist) Above: Daughters of the American Revolution at a celebration in Sussex County. (Larry Fink)

Overleaf: Misses America of the past are enshrined in this banquet room in Atlantic City's Convention Hall. (William Suttle)

INTO THE FUTURE

As New Jersey sets out into the future, it does so with some cause for hope. There is, indeed, a distinct sense of optimism in the air, though not of an inanely boosterish nature. Rather, New Jersey seems—far more than its neighbors—willing and able to face up to some harsh realities. And it is doing something about them.

The state's density of industrial development and density of population (greater even than that of India) have caused major problems with pollution and diminishing wild lands over the years. But it is precisely because of this that New Jersey has become, in effect, a laboratory of environmental problems and their solutions.

Today, New Jersey leads the fifty states in its efforts to protect the air,

Opposite: A landfill in the meadowlands. (Jan Staller) Left: Miss Liberty presides over a collection of ancient wharves. (Henri Cartier-Bresson/MAGNUM)

land, and water. This can be seen in two major endeavors: the cleaning up of toxic-waste dumps, and the development and implementation of land-use legislation. New Jersey's "superfund" program to clean up targeted toxic-waste sites even predates that of the federal government and, along with California's, is one of the top two such programs in the country. Granted, the state does have many dump sites that we know require urgent attention. But, in large, part the number of avowed problem sites reflects the willingness of state politicians, Democrat and Republican alike, to look at the problem squarely. "Seek and ye shall find" is the truest truism of all when it comes to pollution; and since the superfund program was begun in 1976, there has been a startling consistency in its mission to seek. No other comparably endangered state has set up a "search and destroy" team such as New Jersey's. And cleanup is, however slowly, underway. In addition, in recent years the federal Environmental Protection Agency has recorded significant declines of New Jersey's air pollutant levels, especially that of sulfur dioxide, and a decline in many pollution-related diseases as well.

Perhaps the greatest achievement to date of the superfund project has been its alerting and educating of the citizens of the state. An educated and

New Jersey moves into the future with high technology, here embodied in two views of the PA Tech facility in Hightstown. This firm, which specializes in optical, electronic, and semiconductor technology, boasts headquarters by architect Sir Richard Rogers, designer of the Beaubourg in Paris, a fact which accounts for the science-fictional array of ducts. (Both: Otto Baitz)

The lobby of the AT&T building in Basking Ridge seems to spill down in a series of terraces like a hillside garden. (E. R. Degginger)

appropriately outraged citizenry is the best hope for large-scale cleanup in the face of stonewalling by industry. Certainly at this writing it is the only hope for problems such as that of the dumping at Lakehurst's U.S. Naval Air Station.

Meanwhile, New Jersey's land-protection laws have tried, with some success, to keep pace with development. The state's Coastal Zone Management Act is one of the most effective in the country. Instituted in 1972, after much of the coastline was already heavily developed, the success of this program has depended on the fact that it allows for some areas to remain intensely urban while protecting still-wild areas from further encroachment. This kind of mixed-use approach has also been effectively implemented under the similar Delaware River Coast Zone Law.

The Hackensack Meadowlands Protection Law has shaped the sudden growth there, under the watchful eye of the Meadowlands Development Commission in Secaucus. Thus, as sports arenas, racetracks, parking lots, and industrial facilities are built, the water in the Hackensack River actually runs cleaner.

Furthermore, New Jersey has a so-called Green Acres Program designed to help communities preserve whatever open space remains. Under this provision, a town can buy up land to protect it from commercial and

residential development, and the state will cover half the cost.

In spite of all this, of course, New Jersey remains crowded, industrialized, and heavily traveled—a blueprint, as we have said, for the menacing megalopolis. It is impossible to predict the future. Hope and fear clash; now one takes ascendancy, then the other. Certainly in the course of these chapters that has been the case. And something of that ambivalence surely touches all New Jerseyans.

In recent years, there has been a marked improvement in the state's self-image. Bruce Springsteen—who, like all true patriots, can love his homeland and criticize it at the same time—may have had a lot to do with it. Progress in the environment, the relative health of commerce and industry, and the efforts to clean up organized crime have certainly contributed as well. The Eagleton Institute of Rutgers University found in a 1984 survey that 80 percent of residents rated their state as "good" or "excellent"—a considerable increase from seven years earlier, when only 62 percent felt that way.

Significantly, New Jersey leads the way into the future for all of us, according to some scientists, in the ongoing research on nuclear fusion. Nuclear fission is what blows up bombs and fuels the hazardous nuclear power plants around the country; nuclear fusion, not yet practicable for

Michael Graves appears to have been inspired by bathhouse architecture in his design for the Environmental Center at Liberty State Park in Jersey City. (Barry M. Winiker)

Overleaf: A PATH train bound for the World Trade Center awaits commuters in Hoboken. (Jon Eric Jensen)

daily use, holds the promise of generating far greater power at far lower risk. Deep in the well-ordered bowels of the Princeton University Plasma Physics Laboratory, a team of physicists that has been working since the 1950s believes that it is nearing the critical stages of its research. If these scientists succeed, we can only hope that here, in the largest magnetic fusion research facility in the country (and in the same labs where early research was done on the H-bomb), science will produce a tool not for senseless destruction but for peace and prosperity.

On such hopes do all of our futures depend. Yet reaching the future—in New Jersey and everywhere else—requires a realistic understanding of our limits as well as our dreams. There's a home-grown New Jersey myth that seems oddly apropos here, concerning a local troublemaker known as the Jersey Devil. A team of hockey players has been skating under that banner of late, but their namesake is nearly as old as the hills.

In 1735, according to legend, one Mother Leeds of Estelville, in the Pine Barrens, bore her dozenth child. She, feeling no doubt that enough was more than enough, announced to the world at large (and, one imagines, to Father Leeds), "If I ever have another child, may he be a devil." In the next year, she had her thirteenth babe, who emerged from the womb in the shape of a large bird, with cloven hooves and the head of a ram. This ghastly critter flew up the chimney, gathering a glow from the embers that would never die out, and flapped away into the night.

Since then, the Jersey Devil has been seen all over the state, starting fires in the Pine Barrens, stealing livestock, collecting tolls at the Holland Tunnel. In 1939, he was adopted as the official State Beast. There is a price on his head in South Jersey.

What a suggestive story this is, really. That in this most sophisticated of states, a ravening beast should prowl the streets and roofs of Summit, of Short Hills, Bernardsville, Cape May, Glassboro, Elizabeth, Newark, Trenton, and Freehold. Could it be that the Jersey Devil is the flip side of progress? The dark side of birth, growth, industry, and civilization? If so, he has found his true home. Ever let him reign with his rude anarchy, flapping noiselessly over the sands and pines and tract houses, a living embodiment of Wretched Excess.

A state with the irony to embrace such a prodigal son provokes—what else?—a laugh. Yes, but also admiration; and yes, even awe.

This lavish dwelling in Llewellyn is executed in the neo-Babylonian style as it might be imagined on another planet. Here, the indoor pool, shaded by metallic palms, beckons invitingly. (Peter Aaron/ESTO)

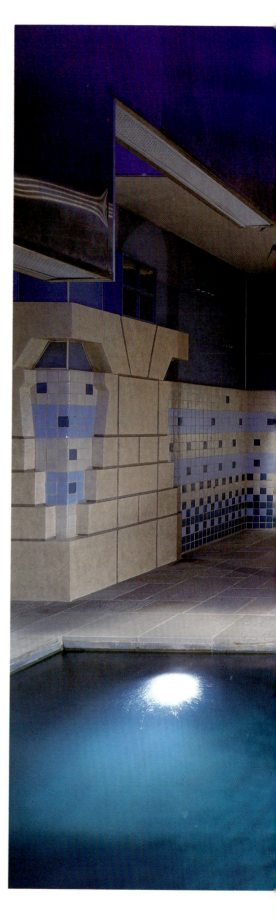

An appropriately dizzying view of one of Action Park's most turbulent rides. (David McGlynn)

New Jersey has taken a leap into the future with its investigation of sea-water conversion, which in not too many years could be the source of most drinking water. One by-product of this industry will be a great deal of salt, as these tableaux suggest. Opposite: A looming mountain of the stuff in Perth Amboy. Left and below: Smaller piles processed in the meadowlands. (All: Jan Staller)

Overleaf: A lyrical view leading down the garden path on the Cross estate in Bernardsville. (Anne Ross)

INDEX

Action Park, 128, 176-177
Agriculture, 55, 61, 63-65, 68, 73-74
Airlines, 16, 23
Airports, 23
Alliance, 40
American Telephone & Telegraph, 170
Amusement parks, 10, 125-128, 176-177
Architecture, 38-39, 42-43, 68, 152-153,
    155, 174-175
Arts, 142
Asbury Park, 10, 37, 107-109, 126-127, 154
Atco Raceway, 132
Atlantic City, 22-23, 105, 108, 112, 114, 115,
    128-129, 142-143
Atlantic City Raceway, 132
Atlantic Highlands, 107
Attitude, 157
Avon-by-the-Sea, 109

Basking Ridge, 40
Bay Head, 111
Bayonne, 40
Bell Labs, 91
Belmar, 109
Berkeley, Lord John, 33
Bernardsville, 40
Bertrand Island Park, 128
Blackledge-Kearny House, Fort Lee, 152
Blueberries, 84, 85
Boundary line, 33, 35
Boxwood Hall, Elizabeth, 152
Bradley Beach, 109
Brendan Byrne Stadium, 132-133
Bridges, 25, 27, 29, 99, 158-159
Brigantine, 111

Camden, 40, 42, 86, 142
Camping, 133
Canals, 76
Canoeing, 75, 133
Cape May, 104, 105, 115, 118-123
Car racing, 132
Carnegie, Andrew, 129
Carteret, Sir George, 33
Casino industry, 115, 128-129, 142-143
Chemical Control Corporation, 86
Chemical explosions, 26, 27, 86, 88-89
Clementon River Park, 128
Coastal Zone Management Act, 170
Coastline, 35, 76, 105-124, 170
College teams, 133
Colleges and universities, 91, 93
Colonia, 40
Communes, 40
Commuters, 24
Congressmen, 49
Corporations, 12-13, 85-86, 168-170
Corruption, 55
Cranberries, 64-65, 101-103
Crops, 63-65, 73, 84, 85, 101-103
Cross estate, Bernardsville, 179-181

Dairy farming, 63
Daughters of the American Revolution, 163
Deal, 32, 40, 107, 108, 110
Delaware River, 75, 152
Dey Mansion, Wayne, 151
Diners, 42-43
Donovan, Raymond, 55
Dunellen, 37

Edison, Thomas, 142, 155, 157
Education, 91, 93
Elizabeth, 40, 86
Employment, 85-104
Englewood, 37
Englishtown Raceway Park, 36, 132, 144-145
Environmental Center, Liberty State Park, 171
Environmental issues, 73, 75, 94, 167,
    169-170
Environmental Protection Agency, 94, 169
Ethnic groups, 33, 36-37, 40, 50-53

Farming, 55, 61, 63-65, 68, 73-74
Fireworks, 100, 101
Fishing, 73, 76, 77, 133
Food production, 68, 73
Ford Mansion, Morristown, 151
Fort Dix, 92, 93
Fort Lee, 40
Fourierist Phalanx, Red Bank, 40
Franklin, Benjamin, 16
Free schools, 91, 93
Freehold Raceway, 132, 136

Garden State Park racecourse, 132
Garden State Parkway, 14, 23
George Washington Bridge, 25
Gilchrist, William Wallace, 142
Giluchow, Elizar, 53
Giorgio's, Hoboken, 57
Glass industry, 78, 151
Golfing, 136
Government, 48-49, 55
Governor, 48
Graves, Michael, 171
Great Adventure, 128
Great Egg Harbor Inlet, 115
Great Falls, Paterson, 2
Green Acres Program, 170

Hague, Frank, 55
Hamilton, Alexander, 157
Heath, Roy, 99
Highlands, 40, 107
Highways, 16, 23, 55, 130
Hiking, 133
Hindenburg, 23, 94
History of New Jersey, 151-166
Hoboken, 34, 37
Hoboken train stations, 5, 29, 148, 161, 171,
    172-173
Hope, 40
Hornblower, Josiah, 155
Horse racing, 132, 136, 137
Hudson, Henry, 151

Impelliteri, Anthony, 55
Indian King Tavern, Haddonfield, 152
Industrial parks, 90
Industry, 12-13, 85-104, 155, 157, 168-170
Inness, George, 142
Intracoastal Waterway, 107
Iron industry, 76, 78, 151, 155, 157
Irvington, 40
Island Beach State Park, 111
Island Swim, 57-59

Jefferson, Thomas, 63, 78
Jersey City, 40, 85
Jockey Hollow, Morristown, 151
Johnson, Robert Gibbon, 63, 78
Jokes, 15, 73

Keansburg, 107
Keyport, 107

Lafferty, James V., 107
Lake Carnegie, 128, 129
Lakehurst Naval Air Engineering Center, 94,
    170
LaSasso, Dan, 101
Lawyers, 87, 90
Leaning Tower of Pizza, 43
Leutze, Emanuel, 152
Lincoln Tunnel entrance, 24
Little Egg Inlet, 111
Livestock, 63, 64
Long Beach Island, 111
Long Branch, 105, 107
Longport, 115
Lucy the Elephant, Margate City, 106, 107

Manasquan, 111
Margate City, 106, 107, 115
Marlborough-Blenheim Hotel, Atlantic City,
    112
Mantoloking, 111
Max Lumber, Jersey City, 86-87
McGuire Air Force Base, 93
McKinley, William, 49
Meadowlands Sports and Recreation Complex,
    132-133, 138-139
Menlo Park, 155, 157
Mercedes-Benz, Montvale, 90, 91
Mercer, Hugh, 163
Military, 93-95
Misses America, 163-165
Monmouth Beach, 107
Monmouth Park racecourse, 132
Moore Estate, Convent Station, 68, 69
Morozoff, Maria, 52
Morris Goodkind Memorial Bridge, 29
Morristown, 151
Motion pictures, 98, 142
Mount Laurel decision of 1985, 55

Native Americans, 151
New Jersey Turnpike, 16
New York City, 19-21
Newark, 37, 40, 86
Newbold, Charles, 64

Nicholson, Jack, 142
North Stelton, 40
Nuclear fusion, 171, 174
Nudism, 136

Ocean City, 40, 115
Ocean Grove, 40, 44-47, 108-109
Old Bridge Raceway, 132
Oldwick, 40

PA Tech, Hightstown, 12-13, 168-169
Palisades Park, 125, 128
Parker, Dorothy, 142
Passaic River, 27, 142
Paterson, 37, 157
Penn, William, 15-16, 33
Picatinny Arsenal, 93
Pillar of Fire Society, 40
Pine Barrens, 36, 62, 75, 76, 78, 80-83, 155, 157
Place names, 157
Point Pleasant, 111
Point Pleasant Beach, 40-41
Politics, 43, 48-49, 55
Pollution, 94, 167, 169-170
Population, 48, 151
Port Elizabeth, 26
Poverty, 40
Princeton, reenactment of Battle of, 162-163
Princeton University, 93, 154, 160
Pulaski Skyway, 19, 23

Railroads, 16-17, 23, 27
Raritan River, 158-159
Red Bank, 40
Red Tower, Plainfield, 56, 57
Revolutionary War, 16, 151-152, 162-163
Ringwood Manor, 68
Rivers, 75-76
Roadhouses, 129-130
Roads, 16
Rockingham House, Rocky Hill, 152
Rogers, Sir Richard, 169
Rosie's Diner, Roselle Park, 42, 43
Rova Farms, Jackson, 40, 52-53
Rumson, 40

Sandy Hook, 107
Santore family, 101
Scotch Plains, 37
Sea Bright, 107
Sea Girt, 111
Seabrook family, 68
Seaside Heights, 111
Sea-water conversion, 178-179
Self-image, 171
Senators, 49
Shore, 35, 76, 105-124, 170
Short Hills, 40
Size of New Jersey, 15
Skiing, 132, 136
Smith, Patti, 142
Smithville Mansion, Mount Holly, 157
South Jersey, 35
Speedwell complex, 157

Sports, 40-41, 124, 132-133, 138-139
Spring Lake, 111
Springsteen, Bruce, 73, 108, 130, 171
Stevens, Colonel John, 16, 155
Stone Harbor, 132
Stone Pony, Asbury Park, 130-131

Teaneck, 37
Tomatoes, 63, 64, 78
Tourism, 136, 142
Trump's Castle, Atlantic City, 142-143
Tuckerton, 111
Turiano, Chester, 101
Typical New Jersey community, 42-43, 48

Unemployment, 86
Union City, 37

Ventnor, 115
Verrazano, Giovanni da, 151

Washington, George, 151-152, 163
Waterfront, 85
Waterloo Village, 156
Wealth, 40
Weehawken, 35, 37
West New York, 37
Whitman, Walt, 142
Wildwood, 115
Williams, Harrison "Pete," 55
Williams, William Carlos, 142
Wilson, Edmund, 142
Wilson, Woodrow, 49
Woodstown, 155
Woolcott, Alexander, 40
Work force profile, 87
Wright brothers, 16

Zarephath, 40
Zoning, 55, 170

PHOTOGRAPHY CREDITS

All photographs are copyrighted in the name of the individual photographers unless otherwise indicated.

Peter Aaron/ESTO, 174-175
Armand Agresti, 16-17, 26-27, 27 top and bottom
Otto Baitz, 12-13, 168-169, 169
Henri Cartier-Bresson/MAGNUM PHOTOS INC., 38-39, 116-117, 167
John Colwell/Grant Heilman Photography, 73 left
Diane Cook, 68, 70-71
William Coupon, 52, 53
E. R. Degginger, 74-75, 102-103, 170
Jim Dow, 138-139
Mitch Epstein, 98 top and bottom
Larry Fink, 15, 96, 137 top, 140 bottom, 163
Jan Groover, 60
Mick Hales, 80 top and bottom, 80-81, 82-83
Grant Heilman/Grant Heilman Photography, 73 right, 113
Tom Herde, 79, 124
Robin Holland, 32
Wolfgang Hoyt/ESTO, 90, 91
Mark R. Jenkinson, 92-93, 94, 95 top and bottom
Jon Eric Jensen, 34-35, 57 top, 172-173
Len Jenshel, 10, 126, 126-127, 142-143
John Kennard, 24, 29 top, 35, 40-41
Bob Krist, 22-23, 50 top and bottom, 51, 72, 75, 77, 84, 88-89, 118, 119, 122-123, 125, 133, 137 bottom, 146-147, 154 top, 162-163
R. Mackson/FPG Int'l., 136
Joe Maloney & Pace/MacGill Gallery, 20-21, 36, 37, 48, 54-55, 61, 64, 65, 109, 130, 130-131, 134-135, 140 top, 141, 150-151, 154 bottom

John Margolies/ESTO, 46-47, 112 top, bottom left and right
David McGlynn, 176-177, 184
Ray Mortenson, 29 bottom, 85
New Jersey Division of Travel & Tourism, 106, 132, 156-157
Peter Ralston, 100-101, 101 top and bottom
Joyce Ravid, 2, 86-87, 144-145
Diane Repp, 45 top left and right, bottom left and right
Curt Richter, 44, 149, 158-159
Ken Robbins, 14 (from City/Country by Ken Robbins, copyright © Ken Robbins, 1985. Reprinted by permission of Viking Penguin, Inc.)
Brian Rose, 25, 148
Anne Ross, 63, 66-67, 69, 180-181
Runk/Schoenberger/Grant Heilman Photography, 62-63
Nancy Sirkis, 28
Michael A. Smith, 128-129, 160 top and bottom (courtesy of the Princeton Gallery of Fine Art)
Jan Staller, 5, 18, 19, 99, 104, 120, 121, 161, 166, 178, 179 top and bottom
Mark Stern, 110-111
Joel Sternfeld, 30-31 (courtesy Daniel Wolf, Inc., New York)
William Suttle, 58-59, 108, 114-115, 164-165
George Tice, 56, 57 bottom, 78, 97, 105, 152, 152-153
Murray Tinkelman, 155
Harvey Wang, 42, 43
Alex Webb/MAGNUM PHOTOS INC., 33
Jeff Weiner, 49
Barry M. Winiker, 171

The parachute ride at Action Park. (David McGlynn)